Perfect Praying

5 Simple Steps That Make Prayers Work

Jon William Lopez, RScP

with

Beatrice Elliott, RScP

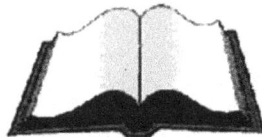

CCB Publishing
British Columbia, Canada

Perfect Praying: 5 simple steps that make prayers work

Copyright ©2007 by Jon William Lopez with Beatrice Elliott
ISBN-13   978-0-9784388-0-7
First Edition

Library and Archives Canada Cataloguing in Publication
Lopez, Jon William, 1952-
Perfect Praying: 5 simple steps that make prayers work / written
by Jon William Lopez; with Beatrice Elliott. – 1st ed.
Also available in electronic format.
ISBN 978-0-9784388-0-7
1. Prayer. I. Elliott, Beatrice, 1946- II. Title.
BL560.L663 2007   204'.3   C2007-905177-4

All photos contained herein including cover image by Jon William Lopez.

Publisher: CCB Publishing
             British Columbia, Canada
             www.ccbpublishing.com

This book is dedicated to my parents, Elaine and Cesar, as well as to my partner, Gray. Through them I know what unconditional love is. I also dedicate this book to my cousin Tina, who first introduced me to New Thought science, and to Reverend Helen Street, who sparked my spirit.

Jon William Lopez, RScP

I dedicate this book to my wonderful Mom, Bernice Austina Underdahl Elliott Jensen.

Beatrice Elliott, RScP

FOREWORD

The power of prayer is more important in our world than ever before. We live in a time when the appearance that "faster and bigger" is better. This notion is compounded with a false belief system that we need to push and force life in order to survive and compete. However this craze and chaos is literally making us sick. All you have to do for a quick fix in your life nowadays is to turn on the tube, and you will find an answer to your woes in a fabricated commercial. "Just take the latest pill," the handsome actors suggest, and you won't be depressed, in pain, without 'love', addicted, fearful or sick ever again... and the list goes on and on.

The truth is that these quick fixes are only a band-aid to someone's well-being. This is where Jon William Lopez and Beatrice Elliott's enlightened book *Perfect Praying* comes in. They write with simplicity and have carefully spelled out a prescription of "Perfect Prayer" that can easily be practiced every day.

They give the reader a 5-step guide to empowering one's self by practicing daily affirmations which can help many people seeking a way to understand and use "prayer" within their lives. They also show how to become more aware of the power of prayer and positive thought and its cause and effect. Each chapter is beautifully illustrated with a photograph of nature which reminds us all that we are connected with a simple order; allowing and trusting, for example, that the rose covered with snow in winter will bloom once again in the spring. If we allow ourselves to be nurtured and do the conscious work, then our lives can change dramatically. We can choose perfect health, we can choose to be grateful, we can change how we look at loss and we can choose kindness and forgiveness.

Jon and Beatrice's book gives us a well-thought-out roadmap to follow but in the end we must all do our own work to achieve what we want out of life. Jon William Lopez and I worked together for many years at the Glendale Church of Religious Science in Glendale, California, where I was Musical Director and he was the Sound Producer. I know prayer practitioner and co-author Beatrice Elliott from the North Hollywood Church of Religious Science in North Hollywood. As a successful cabaret singer, actress and coach to my daughter Katharine McPhee when she appeared on *American Idol*, using the 5 Steps outlined in this book has resulted in many positive demonstrations throughout my life and career.

I personally have been practicing these principles for years and am thrilled that they have written this book.

Inspiration is a beautiful gift!

Blessings, and know that we all have courage to change.

Namaste,

Peisha McPhee
www.peishamcphee.com

ACKNOWLEDGMENTS

Many people have supported me throughout my life experience, contributing to the spiritual journey that has resulted in the publication of this book. I would like to acknowledge my cousins Coppelia, Dagmar, and Zulma, my sisters in Spirit; Reverend Jac Blackman, for his spiritual leadership; Keith Auger for his kindness, wisdom and mentorship; the congregation of the High Desert Center for Spiritual Living, who welcomed my partner and I with open arms; Reverend "Happy" Shaw, who advised me that there are no wrong choices; Marjorie Larragoite, who taught me well; Jacquaeline Hellman, whose prayers are lyric poetry; and Dr. Paul Daniel Payne, who I am convinced is an angel here on Earth.

JWL

PREFACE

The word "God" means different things to different people. For some, it brings up an image of a comforting, humanlike, protective father figure. To others the term connotes a stern, arrogant, judgmental and punishing personality. And to still others, it means a genderless, unconditionally accepting, universal creative power, source of all Life. Whatever name most resonates with you regarding this Higher Power is fine. For simplicity's sake, however, and for the purposes of this book, the term "Spirit" will be used, with a few exceptions here and there as deemed appropriate. I also refer to Spirit as "It", since I believe the Creator to be genderless. As you read and use this book, feel free to use any name or gender you feel most comfortable with.

I sometimes also use the term "Universe", with a capital "U", in the same way as "Spirit", and sometimes "universe" as a physical place, rather than as an aspect of Spirit. This also applies to the use of the term "law". When referring to spiritual "Law" or "Laws" I spell it with a capital "L", while physical "law" or "laws" are spelled with a lowercase "l".

Go with the flow!

JWL

CONTENTS

INTRODUCTION

During a time of seemingly increased uncertainty, violence, insecurity and fear, when more and more people feel they are losing more and more control over their lives and livelihoods, many have turned to conventional or traditional religion in search of comfort, safety and security. They hope to find the sense of wholeness, meaning and well-being that religion promises. As they were taught, they often pray in a meek, needy, supplicating way to a distant, judgmental father-figure God who, depending on the virtue of the individual, may or may not deem to grant his or her request. Furthermore, many people only pray when they want some "thing" or are in desperate trouble.

For an increasing number of others, however, the concept of a traditional "God-figure" is found to be lacking, unfulfilling and even demeaning. Finding traditional prayer, in which one supplicates, pleads or cajoles ultimately unsatisfying, an increasing number of people are searching for ways to speak to and *experience* Spirit in more direct, self-affirming, practical and meaningful ways; to feel Spirit living, moving and having Its being in, through and as them every day.

This book can empower *you* to do exactly that. It is a spiritual yet simple *practical* guide that shows you how to easily compose and create effective prayers that, when stated with conviction and belief, trigger the appropriate universal spiritual Laws which are proven to produce amazing results. This guide outlines the five Steps used in Affirmative Prayer; a positive, proactive, consciously directed, confident and creative statement of fact, and how you can use them to create "perfect" prayers.

Affirmative praying is not supplicating, fear-based or needy. Where traditional prayer solicits a request to a "God-person" that is separate and "out there", hoping for answers, Affirmative Prayer starts with the knowing that Spirit is not only the Creator and Source of all Life, It is *present everywhere* as well as *within* all Life. An Affirmative Prayer recognizes that the Universe (as an aspect and out-picturing of Spirit) always says, "Yes!" and manifests and reflects back to you what you think and say into it. Since Spirit expresses in, through and *as* you, it logically follows that what is true of It must therefore be true of you as well. This includes the creative power of your word, which, as Spirit in expression, is Law in the universe. Using the spiritual Laws of Cause, Attraction, Manifestation and Effect, you manifest your reality and create your experience by what you believe, how you think, and what you say, often unconsciously. Speaking your word unconsciously, day after day, often manifests what might seem like negative results, or provides results that you didn't expect or wish for. The five Steps used in Affirmative Prayer put the spiritual Law of Mind (more on that later) into *conscious*, directed motion, which then manifests as specific form. The Steps transcend all spiritual beliefs, and so they can work for *anyone* of any spiritual tradition, religion or teaching, as well as for anyone of no particular spiritual persuasion as well. Why? Because *it is done unto you AS you believe.*

Social research shows that what you believe, think and say is what shows up in your life. *Perfect Praying: 5 Simple Steps That Make Prayers Work* is intended to be an easy-to-use, non-denominational guide for people across the board who wish to consciously participate and become *co-creators* with Spirit. It puts the "positive punch" into prayer.

To quote Abe Lincoln, "I think people are about as happy as they make up their minds to be." This guide allows you to "re-mind" with your positive, powerful SELF.

CHAPTER ONE

THE POWER OF THOUGHT

Do you pray? Even if you don't think you do, you do. Even if you don't believe in a God, Spirit or Higher Power, you do because every thought you think, every statement you make, and every belief you hold is a form of prayer that "answers" you back by attracting into your life or manifesting outwardly as some form of physical thing, outcome, situation, circumstance or condition. Whether you believe this or not, whether you are conscious of this or not, your word is Law in the universe!

Those of you who do pray in a more traditional manner, if even occasionally, may sometimes feel that your prayers don't really work, or seldom the way you'd like them to. Do you often get the answers or the results you seek? If not, it may be because of the *way* you are praying, to an individualized, judgmental God that is *out there* and separate from you, to whom you are petitioning in fear, need and doubt, attempting to win his favor with contrition, promises and persuasion.

As a matter of fact, Spirit, or whatever term feels most comfortable to you, is not an individual personality separate and apart from you, but is an infinite, Intelligent Creative *Principle*, Power and Force that perfectly expresses and lives in, through and as you! As an expression of Spirit, what is true of It is true of you. Therefore your word, on an individual level, like Spirit's on a universal level, is Law in the universe. *Your* universe. It has power. Because of this, every statement you make or thought you have, based on your innermost beliefs, sets into motion certain spiritual Laws which manifest in one form or another. When you speak your word, whether in focused, directed prayer or through simple everyday statements, you put into motion the spiritual Laws of Cause, Attraction and Manifestation/Effect. These Laws or Principles are as real as any laws of physics, and work just as predictably, scientifically and, in a sense, as *mechanically* as any physical law. Every thought you have or statement you make (cause) triggers a physical or energetic reaction (attraction), which results in a physical form (manifestation) or outcome (effect). The world of physical reality around you – and in you – is, in fact, the accumulation of an infinite number of effects created by an infinite number of underlying causes, stretching back through time. Your very life, right now, is the effect, or result, of your beliefs, thoughts, words, actions and *re*-actions which over time have manifested as your reality and have created your experience.

Why? Because *what you believe to be true, you attract into your life*. This is the Law of Attraction, and your use of it is often unconscious. This happens because the Universe is an intelligent spiritual system that does not judge or play favorites. It is neutral and impartial, giving back equally to all. It always says "Yes!" automatically out-picturing back to you *everything* you think into it, positive or negative, whether you're aware of it or not.

It should also be said, however, that although everything happens through you, seemingly unforeseen events also can, and do, sometimes impact you from the "outside", apparently from out of left field and over which you seem to have no control. It is how you interpret, think about, respond to, and deal with these seemingly unexpected events, however, that makes the difference. What you believe, think, say and do about them determines the effect they ultimately have on your life and how they will shape your experience.

So, just imagine now how your life might look if you were always *aware* of the power your beliefs, thoughts and words had to create your experience, and of your *ability to use that power!* Wishful thinking? Absolutely not. This book is a *practical* guide to facilitate you into bringing your *un*-conscious thinking, speaking and *praying* into the light of *conscious awareness* and *proactive direction.* As such, every thought you think and every word you speak out-pictures as your perfect reality and attracts your good in a powerful, positive manner that *you* create, no longer a seeming "victim" of circumstances. As a perfect expression of Spirit, a happy, healthy, love-filled, prosperous and fulfilling life is your natural birthright. The five Steps of Affirmative Prayer described and exemplified here will move you down a clear, smooth and fulfilling path that allows you to create, according to your faith and belief, the kind of life *you* choose.

CHAPTER TWO

AFFIRMATIVE PRAYER

What is prayer, exactly?

According to Webster's definition, a prayer is, "An address (as a petition) to God or a god in word and thought. An earnest request or wish."

Affirmative Prayer, on the other hand, is a focused, positive, mental process of directed thought into the Universal Mind, wherein certain spiritual Laws are put into motion to attract or manifest a certain outcome, condition or thing. Affirmative Prayer is not a petition, wish or a request, an act of overcoming a fickle God's reluctance, but a conscious *knowing* of your oneness with Spirit and Its complete and total willingness to give that which is already yours by Divine birthright. Spirit, being All There Is, is *unlimited* supply, abundance, perfect solution, happiness and health, and you can partake of it now. It is an awareness that the good of Life is, and always has been, yours. Affirmative Prayer is a conscious conjoining and co-creation with the Spirit within you, that *is* you, to manifest that which *already exists* as a perfect blueprint in Infinite Mind, and is yours to claim and bring forth into immediate manifestation.

Affirmative Prayer is *not* willing something to happen. It opens within you a channel through which it *can* happen. The "Force" is always at work! When you pray affirmatively, you do not send out a petition, request or make a wish – *you realize, reveal and attract the truth, perfection and abundance that is already there.* You set into motion an idea that goes into Infinite Intelligence, where it is accepted at its own level and acted upon.

Prayer *always* works, one way or the other, but sometimes appears to not bring about the particular results you intended or hoped for because of the underlying beliefs with which it was expressed. Traditional, non-affirmative prayer is often an entreaty, with the hope, rather than the *certainty*, that whatever is asked for will be granted. It comes from a belief in separation, a God that is "out there" somewhere. It arises out of a consciousness of lack and an ignorance of the truth that Spirit is *not* separate from you, but is a Creative Power *within* you (as well as all around you). Results from this often fear-based, self-effacing form of prayer can therefore be mixed and unclear. It may not seem to be working, when in fact it actually is. Fear, negativity and doubt result in fear, negativity and doubt. Suffering is not a pre-ordained condition of Life nor is it imposed upon you. It is the result of ignorance of your oneness with Spirit, which is only good, and of the spiritual Laws which run the universe.

A very important reason why your prayers may sometimes not seem to "work" is that Spirit can only do *for* you what It can do *through* you. Spirit reveals and gives to you *only to the degree that you believe It can.* Higher Power cannot work for you until you first recognize It *as* Power. Believe in and expect a little, and you will get a little. Believe in and expect a lot, and your world will be filled with abundance. You may not always get what you want, but you will almost always get what you expect! *Prayer and belief are very closely related.* Faith and belief are the fuel that *powers the prayer!* This is discussed in greater detail later in this guide.

Affirmative Prayer comes from a recognition and awareness of a oneness with the universe, with Life, with Spirit, with Cosmic Consciousness and Infinite Intelligence. What Spirit is in the macrocosm, *you* are in the microcosm, individualized. The Power that created the universe and keeps it eternally in motion is the same Power that created and lives in you, through you, as you and *is you.* Just as an entire image exists on a tiny piece cut from the full portion of a holographic film, *all* of Spirit is within you *in Its totality*. It is everywhere and *equally* present, as It is everywhere and equally present within all creation. That's because at the level of the Absolute, there is no "space". Space is a manifestation of the outer, physical universe. And since in Spirit there is no space, there is no "time" either. Time is an abstract human-created concept for measuring movement *through* space, and only seems to exist because you have a mind which can remember the "past" and can imagine a "future". In fact, there is only the ever-present "now". This is why, once an Affirmative Prayer is released into the Law of Mind, it becomes a done deal, a perfect spiritual/mental blueprint awaiting manifestation; it might just *seem* to take a little "time", on *this* heavier physical plane, to actually manifest.

There is a Power for the Positive in the universe. As an expression of Spirit you have the ability to use it! The universe is unlimited abundance, lacking nothing. Everything is already available to you, and all that is necessary to have it is to declare it into physical manifestation through the power of your thoughts, words and the right use of spiritual Laws.

You already live in a perfect universe. Simply perceive and recognize it mentally and it will become part of your experience.

CHAPTER THREE

THE LAWS OF MIND:
CAUSE, ATTRACTION &
MANIFESTATION/EFFECT

Prayers work because they set into motion certain universal spiritual Principles which, when fully comprehended, can be consciously and proactively used and directed. Just as there are unseen but very real scientifically measurable laws of physics which propel and govern the physical universe, there are also underlying, unseen, and *very real scientifically measurable* spiritual Laws which move and govern all of Life and Creation. Perhaps the most significant and powerful of these Principles is the Law of Mind and as aspects of it, the Laws of Cause, Attraction and Manifestation/Effect.

The Law of Mind is an aspect of Spirit which, although intelligent, is not conscious and has no volition of its own. It is triggered by our thoughts and words, mechanically taking them and transforming them into a form, situation, condition, circumstance, outcome or event. It takes what it receives *literally, impartially and without judgment.* Allowed to work without interference, it manifests *exactly* what is thought into It.

The Law of Cause is what the Infinite Intelligence or Mind of Spirit brings into action. In Spirit, it is the Word or Divine Idea, backed by intention or desire. Spirit is the ultimate First Cause of all creation. In us, Cause is triggered by our own ideas, intentions or desires, and molded by our beliefs, thoughts or statements.

Immediately following Cause, the Law of Attraction is set into motion as soon as a thought or statement, backed by belief and intention, is expressed. This Law has a "magnetic" effect, and its nature is to attract (rather than to create from nothing) people, situations or things to you that may already exist. Once an intention is expressed, the Law of Attraction begins arranging the ways and means for your intention to be fulfilled, pulling in the necessary circumstances, opening the right doors, providing the perfect opportunities, people and things into your sphere of reality, often from what might seem to be out of thin air!

Working in conjunction with the Law of Attraction is the Law of Manifestation, and they might sometimes be perceived as one and the same. Both are the natural consequence of the Law of Cause. The Law of Manifestation (like the Law of Attraction) takes the "seed" (thought) that is planted by you and makes it sprout (manifest). When allowed to perform its function without interference, such as another thought or statement canceling out the first one, the Law of Manifestation literally and exactly takes the mental equivalent of whatever was thought into it and transforms it into physical form.

As mentioned earlier, it would not be inaccurate to say that all form, all Life, the entire manifest universe around you is, at its core, a gigantic and ever-changing series of Effects, the result of an incalculable, mind-boggling number of Causes, stretching back into infinity. What seems solid and permanent is, on an infinite universal scale, a transitory, temporary condition. You, or at least your body, is the Effect of an underlying mental and spiritual Cause, Spirit. The physical you is patterned after, and is the resulting out-picturing of, a whole, perfect blueprint (Cause) in the Mind of Spirit. In fact, all physical disease is the Effect, and as such has no power in and of itself, of an underlying condition of "dis-ease" or negative belief and emotions within. Seemingly "outside" causes of illness such as germs or viruses are also simply the Effects of other Causes which can impinge upon you. It is the consciousness within – and particularly the *race consciousness* of humankind – that harbors a *belief* in sickness or allows for the *possibility* or *idea* of it that allows external agents or illness to intrude and take hold.

Effects are the natural and inevitable consequences of the Laws of Cause, Attraction and Manifestation being allowed to follow through to their natural completion. These Laws are constantly in motion, flowing, interacting and weaving the infinite tapestry of the universe, reality and experience. In Affirmative Praying, learning to use these Laws is more a question of understanding, and then *allowing* them to work rather than in knowing *how* they work. Once set into motion, they need no help from you, and will carry out their functions through to their logical perfect outcome unless re-directed or aborted. Simply being conscious of these Principles and knowing what they do and how you can use them is sufficient. No task, no desire, no request and no issue is too difficult or too large for them (or Spirit) to handle, for it is these Principles which manifest and keep the universe ticking and forever renewing itself.

Some individuals not familiar with New Thought spiritual practices have the mistaken perception that there is too much emphasis put on manifesting purely material things, with not enough attention given to more non-material, altruistic human issues like love, world peace, world hunger, etc. It might seem that way, but the reason is simply because for us here in the physical world, our everyday practical needs and concerns often seem more immediate and pressing. You cannot meet the needs of the world until you first meet your own. And for those of you who may be new to the concept of Affirmative Prayer and are still learning, manifesting a physical object or condition in your own life might seem to be easier to handle at first, being, as it were, "closer to home". Spirit, however, being Infinite and being All, knows nothing of big or small, material or non-material. It only knows to say "Yes!" and to reflect back that which is thought into It, whether it be a rubber ducky, more money, that new job, perfect health or world peace. Remember, where *you* are concerned, you get to tell the Law of Mind what to do! Once you become confident in your ability to manifest the material things and you feel ready to tackle world peace, then go for it. The more people focused on the higher good, *where two or more are gathered,* the more powerful the results become!

Praying for non-material outcomes is done exactly the same way and with the same degree of faith, conviction and belief, as you would for a rubber ducky or a new job. You need to create just as firm a mental image or idea of your desired outcome as you would for a raise in salary. Instead of imagining what it would be like to *have* something, however, *feel* what it would be like to *be* – or *be in* – the particular situation, condition or circumstance you desire. Feel what it would be like to *be* in good health, have well-being, in a world at peace, and so on. Feel it, and then *act as if it is so* in everything you do.

Because whether you are praying for that new job, house, relationship or an end to world hunger, it's all an "inside" job!

CHAPTER FOUR

STEP 1: RECOGNITION – "SPIRIT IS"

Step 1 is the recognition that there is only one Power, one Source and one Intelligence in the universe. It created the universe and *is* the Universe (with a capital "U"), all in one. It is Spirit, God, Goddess, Source, Creator, Higher Power, Divine Mind, Cosmic Consciousness, Infinite Intelligence, the Force or whatever term you feel most comfortable with. (One minister I knew called It "Big Sweetie!") Whatever you choose to call It, Spirit is everywhere, in everything, and It is *all* there is. All of creation is but a manifestation, out-picturing, expression, extension or effect of It. Nothing is separate from It because everything is made *of* It. It is all of Life and It is the creator of Life, seen and unseen.

In Affirmative Prayer, the idea of the Divine is that Spirit is a creative Principle, not a personality. This means that Spirit is neither male nor female. It is not an old man with a beard sitting up on some lofty heavenly throne looking down, passing judgment or casting plagues upon the world. Such concepts were the creations of a simpler, more limited-thinking people who could not yet conceive of higher forms of expression, and needed their Higher Power to take on a more comfortable, recognizable and anthropomorphic human appearance. Spirit is, in fact, an Intelligent creative Force that works in and through all Life equally, impartially and *impersonally*. (It rains on the sinner and saint alike.) Like electricity, pure Spirit simply *is*, and can be used for positive and negative purposes by everyone, with the corresponding consequences. This is what is meant by the statement "the Universe always says *yes.*" Like an infinite, intelligent mirror, It reflects back to you exactly what you think into It, even though you may not be aware of It. This is discussed in greater detail in Step 3.

Now, the idea of Spirit as a neutral, impersonal universal "Force" might leave you cold. However, Spirit becomes personal through *you* and how you choose to experience and/or believe in It. Giving It a name or an image that feels comfortable is a good way to personalize It for you. Envisioning *your* Higher Power as a favorite hero or character that holds special significance for you is another way. I even heard of someone who envisioned Spirit as the Marlboro Man! Someone else chose to see It as her dearly departed grandmother. If a warm fuzzy "God" is what you need, go for it. If, however, the idea of an omnipotent universal Power like electricity makes more sense to you, then have at it. Do whatever works. Just keep in mind that underneath whatever name or image you choose, and which immediately limits It, exists the omnipresent creative spiritual *Principle* that *unconditionally* works in you, through you, as you and *for* you.

Despite appearances to the contrary, the universe is in fact a place of perfect harmony and order, run by the Cosmic Consciousness that created it. Yes, Virginia, there *is* an Intelligent Designer! But again, It is not some elderly bearded Architect in the Sky sitting at a heavenly drafting table and drawing out blueprints (at least not literally). As discussed previously, the universe is run by spiritual Principles which, no matter what the prevailing theories of the time might be, remain ever constant and never change. When dealing with a Principle, you will always get the same result. A simple example is how mixing certain colors will always produce certain other colors, i.e. blue and yellow make green. This is because while intelligent in nature, spiritual Principles are also mechanical in that they have no volition of their own, and are set into motion only by the Intelligence of Spirit and by you, an individualization of It. Once triggered, their nature is to perform their function automatically.

The purpose of Step 1 is to set the stage for your Affirmative Prayer. It establishes the context and opens your consciousness for the next four Steps to follow. After acknowledging that "Spirit Is", again, using whatever name is most comfortable for you, it is useful to also include at this point some of the qualities or aspects of Spirit that you are praying for. For example, if you are praying for prosperity, you might state that not only is Spirit all there is, It is also unlimited prosperity, abundance, creativity, opulence, supply, etc.

Once you have recognized and established that Spirit is the Creator of all there is, *is* all there is, lives *within* and expresses *as* all there is, and possesses the aspects or qualities you are praying for, you are ready to move on to Step 2.

Here is an example of Step 1, in this case for perfect health:

There is only one Universal Power,
one Infinite Intelligence, one Divine Mind.
It is Spirit, God, Cosmic Consciousness
and It is the Source of all creation.
Spirit is everywhere present, perfectly manifesting,
out-picturing and expressing in, through and as all Life.
It is perfect physical health, unhindered flow,
vibrant energy and perfect wholeness and harmony.

CHAPTER FIVE

STEP 2: UNIFICATION – "I AM"

Step 2 continues by recognizing *your* oneness with Spirit. All Spirit is, you are. There is no separation. It is your source, and you are Its perfect expression. What is true of It is true of you, especially the power of your beliefs, thoughts and words to create your experience and manifest your reality. You and Spirit are co-creators!

Once you recognize, accept and affirm that this Higher Power is the Source of all Life and that It perfectly out-pictures and expresses in, through and *as* all Life, it then follows that *you, as a conscious living being,* must therefore also be a part of It. You and the "Force" are One! You are Spirit-stuff in physical form! There is no separation, nor can there be. In order for you to be alive, Infinite Intelligence must also be *in* you, working *through* you and *as* you, just as electricity must run through the wire and inhabit the bulb if there is to be light. Spirit is your Source, your Creator, and what is true of It on an infinite scale, is true of you on an individualized human scale.

Getting in touch with and experiencing this oneness is as simple (although perhaps not easy at first) as going within yourself and finding that deep, inner place of perfect, quiet consciousness, beyond the mind chatter. That state where you listen from, with and to the heart. It is the still, silent "voice" within called Instinct. Instinct is the voice of Spirit, your true voice, your direct line to the Universe, and It is never wrong. With practice you will learn to recognize It, listen to It, and over time, trust It.

Reaching this place of stillness is achieved with patience and practice. While sitting or lying in a quiet, comfortable place, slow deep breathing or repeating a mantra to yourself are two effective ways to relax and quiet your mind so that you can recognize your oneness with and experience the One Mind. Setting aside a specific time every day and creating a relaxing environment in which to meditate are also conducive to tuning into the Spirit within. Be assured however that by using the 5 Steps, an effective Affirmative Prayer can be done anywhere, at any time. Simply recognizing and affirming your oneness with Spirit with conviction is enough, no matter where you are.

Here is an example of Step 2, again for perfect health:

Recognizing that Spirit is all there is,
I therefore recognize my oneness with It and with all creation.
There is no separation. What is true of Spirit is true of me.
Spirit lives, moves and has Its Being in me, through me,
as me and IS me. Spirit is my Creator, my Source and
my perfect wholeness, health and well-being.

CHAPTER SIX

STEP 3: DECLARATION – "I AFFIRM"

Step 3 follows by declaring or speaking your word (what you wish to manifest) affirmatively, with faith, conviction and in the present tense, stating the good or outcome you desire *as if it were already so*. It is stating in a positive, even *firm* manner, if necessary, what it is you desire from the place of knowing, that you and Spirit are One, and that what is true of It must therefore be true of you. Spirit's nature is your nature. Spirit's Mind is your mind expressing as you, and so you can use It to create whatever outcome you desire. An invisible spiritual Substance surrounds you (it *is* you), and is waiting to be formed. And since Infinite Intelligence can create anything out of Itself, and It is who you are, you have the ability to "think" into reality your experience and the kind of life you desire.

However, since the Universe can only reflect back to you what you think into It, It can only do *for* you what you think and believe it can. Since Spirit will never impose Its will upon you, despite what you may have been taught, you in essence tell *Spirit* what to do whenever you speak your word! So, the more you believe your Higher Power can do for you, the more It will. The more conscious you are of It, the more powerfully you can use It. No matter what you name It, Spirit is an impersonal, impartial Force that works like electricity – you guide It as you see fit, to either shock you or to turn on the lights. The more *aware* you are of Its ability to respond to you to the extent that you believe It will, the greater your results will be.

We discussed earlier the Laws of Cause, Attraction, Manifestation and Effect. As the thinker, you are the Cause in *your* life, and whatever manifests is the Effect. Your life as it is at this very moment is the effect of a myriad of causes, conscious and unconscious, that you have created or that have impacted you. So the more conscious you are of the thoughts and beliefs you hold and their power to create what happens in your life, the more control you can have over their outward Effect.

When in Step 3, use as many affirmative statements that embody your desired outcome or goal as you like. It is important during this Step to establish in your mind, and therefore Spirit's Mind, a strong, clear picture or mental prototype of what you are praying for. See the situation, outcome, condition or thing you are praying for as an *already created* idea, circumstance or object in Divine Mind. *Feel* what it would be like to already actually *have* or *be* what you are praying for, *now,* while you're praying for it!

It is also important during this third Step, and in your everyday thinking for that matter, to declare and focus on what you *do* want, not on what you *don't*. Besides belief, wording is of the utmost importance in prayer since the Law of Mind, being mechanical in nature, *always takes you literally!* Your subconscious mind cannot determine true from false, real from unreal. So, for example, rather than stating "I am no longer sick/I don't want to be ill" or "I am no longer poor," declare that "I am perfect health!" and "I am prosperous in all ways now!" Then *imagine* what good health or prosperity feels like. Wallow in the feeling of well-being and peace of mind that perfect health or prosperity creates within you!

Once you feel satisfied or complete, go on to the next Step.

Here is an example of Step 3 for perfect health:

And so in this consciousness of oneness,
I speak my word, recognizing that it is the word of Spirit.
I know, declare and affirm that I am
perfect health and vitality now.
As Spirit in perfect expression, I am perfect mind and perfect
body, up against which no imperfection or dis-ease can stand.
Any dis-ease or imperfection is now gently, lovingly,
yet completely and permanently released.
My body is patterned after a perfect blueprint in Divine Mind,
and this perfection re-asserts and imprints itself in me,
as me and is me now.
Every atom, molecule, cell, tissue, fiber
and organ of my being is saturated in the perfect healing
power, light and energy of Spirit.
I am healthy, whole and complete now and always.

CHAPTER SEVEN

STEP 4:
THANKSGIVING – "I AM GRATEFUL"

Step 4 is the process of giving thanks *for the good you know is already so.* It is an act of faith. As a neutral, impartial, unlimited and all-giving Intelligence, Spirit does not "need" your gratitude. What a concept! Giving thanks is strictly for your own benefit, to increase your confidence and *trust* in the limitless abundance of the Universe and Its willingness *and ability* to manifest for you. Giving thanks is a "vote of confidence" for the Universe. It is an acknowledgment that your prayer is already a "done deal".

A consciousness of gratitude is an important state of mind, not only in prayer, but in daily living. It assumes that the goodness (or "Godness") of Life is a given and that Spirit is on your side. It establishes a channel through which your good is able to flow easily, effortlessly and constantly. Very simply, an attitude of gratitude *increases* your flow of good.

Again, Spirit does not need or require your gratitude. Your thanks, just like forgiveness, are for your *own* consciousness. Giving thanks shows that you are aware of, recognize, trust and acknowledge the given truth of Spirit's ability and willingness to manifest for you, always. And it reminds you to never take the abundance of the universe for granted.

Here is an example of Step 4:

Thank you Spirit. I am deeply grateful for this truth,
for I know my word is heard even before it is spoken,
and is even now a perfect idea in Divine Mind.
I accept this good, knowing it is already mine now,
and I am filled with thanksgiving.

CHAPTER EIGHT

STEP 5: RELEASE – "I LET GO"

Releasing your prayer into the Universe and letting Spirit take care of it is Step 5, the final Step of an Affirmative Prayer. You've stated your desire and expressed your gratitude. Now, in Step 5, you release your word into the Law of Mind which, if allowed to work undisturbed, takes care of the rest. This means going about your business and letting the seed you have planted have a chance to take root, grow and manifest.

In releasing your prayer, you are again expressing confidence and trust. You are triggering the Law of Mind into action, giving It the go-ahead. You are also affirming to yourself that there is no need to dwell on or worry about *how* or *when* your desired result will manifest, or *if* it will. Release implies that your good is already as good as done and you await its manifestation with joyful anticipation and expectancy.

Be patient, however. Some demonstrations do not happen overnight. Although your desired outcome may already be an instantaneous, perfect idea in Cosmic Consciousness, it sometimes takes "time", from our three-dimensional earthly point of view, for it to manifest on the physical plane. Give the universe time to arrange matters for you! It's a big place and there's a lot going on. Releasing is a way of showing your patience and *trusting* that there will be a result without the need to go back and dig up the seed you've planted to see if it's growing.

Once you have released, *act as if your demonstration has already happened*. This allows you to feel what you would experience if you had already manifested your desire. It is again an acknowledgment that your good is yours now. "Acting as if" fools the subconscious, which does not know the difference between fact and fantasy, and accelerates the Law of Attraction/Manifestation. However, by saying "act as if" I am not suggesting you go out and charge up your credit cards and get into debt just because you have prayed for financial prosperity. Use your common sense.

Remember, *how and when* your demonstration will come about is none of your business. It's Spirit's. Don't worry about it!

Here is an example of Step 5 for perfect health:

And so with the total, indisputable and steadfast faith and trust
of Spirit Itself, I release my word into the Law of Mind,
where through Cosmic Consciousness and Infinite Intelligence
it is immediately, easily and effortlessly manifested
in perfect right timing and order
for my highest and greatest good.
I declare it done. And so it is!
(You may also add "amen" after this if you choose.)

❖

Putting all the Steps together, here is what the entire Affirmative Prayer – in this example for perfect health – looks like:

There is only one Universal Power,
one Infinite Intelligence, one Divine Mind.
It is Spirit, God, Cosmic Consciousness
and It is the Source of all creation.
Spirit is everywhere present, perfectly manifesting,
out-picturing and expressing in, through and as all Life.
It is perfect physical health, unhindered flow,
vibrant energy and perfect wholeness and harmony.

Recognizing that Spirit is all there is,
I therefore recognize my oneness with It and with all creation.
There is no separation. What is true of Spirit is true of me.
Spirit lives, moves and has Its Being in me, through me,
as me and IS me. Spirit is my Creator, my Source and
my perfect wholeness, health and well-being.

And so in this consciousness of oneness,
I speak my word, recognizing that it is the word of Spirit.
I know, declare and affirm that I am
perfect health and vitality now.
As Spirit in perfect expression, I am perfect mind and perfect
body, up against which no imperfection or dis-ease can stand.
Any dis-ease or imperfection is now gently, lovingly,
yet completely and permanently released.
My body is patterned after a perfect blueprint in Divine Mind,
and this perfection re-asserts and imprints itself in me,
as me and is me now.
Every atom, molecule, cell, tissue, fiber
and organ of my being is saturated in the perfect healing
power, light and energy of Spirit.
I am healthy, whole and complete now and always.

Thank you Spirit. I am deeply grateful for this truth,
for I know my word is heard even before it is spoken,
and is even now a perfect idea in Divine Mind.
I accept this good, knowing it is already mine now,
and I am filled with thanksgiving.

And so with the total, indisputable and steadfast faith and trust
of Spirit Itself, I release my word into the Law of Mind,
where through Cosmic Consciousness and Infinite Intelligence
it is immediately, easily and effortlessly manifested
in perfect right timing and order
for my highest and greatest good.
I declare it done. And so it is!

Chapter Nine

The Silent Step

There is actually another Step in this process, one which might be called the Silent Step, but which runs through and underlies all five Steps and is probably the most important one when it comes to determining the quality, strength and outcome of your prayer. This is the *feeling, conviction* or *belief* with which you speak your word, and the *faith* you have in its perfect outcome. Faith, conviction and belief give your prayer power and strength, and determine the quality of the results you receive. Remember, it is done unto you as you *believe*, and so the more heartfelt and confident your prayer is, the "better" your physical demonstration will be. Strong faith and belief are the fuels that propel your prayer into Mind. The more *trusting* you are of the Universe's unlimited potential, and Its ability to always respond to you *to the extent that you believe It will*, the greater your results become. But you must not only have faith in Spirit, you need to also have confidence in your *own ability* and *approach* to It in order for your prayer to be its most effective. You need to believe your word is powerful. This is where the "acting as if" discussed in Step 5 can be most effective!

If you have difficulty feeling confident at first, or if your belief is weak, then do as a very wise and down-to-earth New Thought minister I knew (the one who called Spirit "Big Sweety") once advised: *just say the words.* They have power, no matter what the belief behind them might be. If at first they sound weak and unconvincing to you, your words will eventually, as you steadily see the results they bring, gain strength and truthfulness in your mind until you can utter them with the utmost conviction and without a trace of doubt.

In the beginning you may feel as if some issues are too big or difficult or heavy for you to pray for, and this can indeed affect your faith. Higher Power, however, knows nothing of "big" or "little", "easy" or "difficult". In Spirit, where there is no time or space, it is just as effortless to create a planet as it is to manifest a rubber ducky. But Spirit can manifest for *you* only as much as you believe It can. So if it feels more manageable, begin with something "small" or "easy" (a rubber ducky might be a good starting point), and gradually expand your declarations to larger issues and intentions. Remember to give your prayers "time" to manifest on the physical plane. Be patient with yourself and with the Universe.

In praying, *faith* in perfect outcome, in Spirit's presence and ability, is essential. Faith is a conviction that all is well, that your life is a part of Spirit's, and that It is *on your side, always working for you*. If at first you feel that your faith is not strong enough (or non-existent), if you doubt your trust in Spirit's ability to manifest for you, try coming from the faith *of Spirit* rather than your own. With Spirit, there's never any issue about faith, belief or conviction. In Higher Power, these qualities are givens, whole and complete, unchanging, and never in question. It is only we, on a human scale, who doubt. Leaning on the faith and relying on the trust *of Spirit*, we take the pressure off ourselves and let the Divine take charge. It is actually quite freeing and gets you out of your own way. When you pray, don't feel as if *you* have to do all the work; praying should not feel like work anyway. Let Spirit take over, knowing that the Law of Mind is always in operation. *How* your good comes to you is none of your concern. That is the Law's job, not yours. Once your sincere intention is put out there, the Universe rearranges Itself and provides you with exactly the right ways and means for your desire to manifest. From sometimes the most unexpected sources doors will be opened, opportunities will present themselves, actions to take and paths to follow will be revealed. All easily, effortlessly and in ways that you can clearly see, know, understand and implement.

With the faith and confidence *of Spirit* you can pray with certainty, despite what the present outward physical appearance, situation or condition might be. In Affirmative Prayer you turn away from the outer appearance, the circumstance, the dis-ease. You do not deny it, but recognize it for the *effect* it is, then focus always on the desired ideal, knowing that it is the *real* Truth you seek to reveal. All healing, in fact, is a *revealing*, the clearing away of the fog of effect to uncover or reveal the *underlying* perfection that has always been there.

The Universe brings you what you *expect*. As your use of the five Steps becomes easier and your demonstrations reflect your strengthening faith in yourself and in Spirit, you will come to expect perfect, positive results rather than merely hoping for them.

Take it in baby steps. Have patience, but have confidence. Go about your business and give the seed you have planted time to grow. Gradually, as your demonstrations increase in quantity and quality, your faith, confidence and trust in this profound Divine Process will grow and deepen. As for how long you should treat for something, the answer is simple – until you get your desired outcome!

Remember: the more convinced you are of the power of your own word, the more power your word will have!

Chapter Ten

Composing the
Perfect Prayer

Now that you've learned and have been given examples of what the five Steps are, what they do, and how they go together, you're ready to begin composing Affirmative Prayers of your own. Doing so is stimulating, fulfilling and fun. It is speaking to, and co-creating with Spirit!

In the next chapter are examples of affirmative statements to be used within Step 3 from the five main categories that seem to be of most concern in people's lives: 1) Health, 2) Abundance, Money and Prosperity, 3) Love and Friendship, 4) Work, Self-Expression and Creativity, and 5) Loss. Use these statements verbatim, revise them or as springboards towards creating your own. Wherever "Spirit" or any other term is used, use whatever name you feel most comfortable with.

To begin, choose a category to be used within Step 3 that you would like to address. Then, from that particular category choose an affirmative statement that resonates with you. Next, select statements from Steps 1, 2, 4 and 5 that most relate to the issue you have chosen, and which resonates with you. If you wish, choose a transition statement to insert between Steps 2 and 3.

Write down the statements you have chosen in the appropriate order, i.e. Steps 1 through 5, to create your prayer. You can write your prayer on a single sheet of paper, decorative stationery or on note cards. If you feel so inclined, you may wish to copy down all the statements printed in the next chapter, or create your own using these as a guide, onto individual 3x5 index cards or smaller-sized sheets of loose leaf paper which often come with a binder. With each statement on a separate card or sheet of paper, you can then organize them into their appropriate Steps and categories. This will allow you to mix and match, composing an Affirmative Prayer that is tailored just for you, and that you can change every day.

Displaying the cards on a small picture-frame easel that you can keep on a desk, dresser or personal altar is also a nice touch. A mini photo album, folding credit card wallet or blank diary are other easy, portable ways you can organize or take your assembled prayer with you to refer to wherever and whenever you wish.

Once composed, speak or think your prayer silently to yourself with confidence, faith, conviction and strength, believing that the results you desire have already manifested, that your good is here now, and is yours by Divine birthright! Do this as often as you feel you need to, until you feel complete and at peace. Then release the prayer and go about your business, expecting perfect results.

CHAPTER ELEVEN

STEP STATEMENTS

STEP 1 – RECOGNITION – "SPIRIT IS"

➤ Spirit (or your name for It) is all there is.

➤ Spirit is all there is. It is everywhere and equally present.

➤ There is only one Universal Mind, Creator and Source of all Life.

➤ There is only one Power, Spirit, Infinite Intelligence and Creative Source in the universe, and It manifests in, through and as all Life.

➤ There is only one Source, one Spirit, one Universal Intelligence and one Life. All creation is this Higher Power in perfect expression.

➤ There is only one loving Infinite Spirit, Source of all creation, which lives, moves and has Its Being in, through and as all Life.

➤ There is one Presence and Power in the universe. This Presence is Spirit. It is all there is, everywhere and equally present.

➤ Spirit is everywhere and in everything. It is unconditional love, eternal life, perfect health, unlimited prosperity and supply, and joyous expression.

➤ There is only one Divine Mind, Universal Consciousness and Infinite Intelligence. This Intelligence is Spirit, and it expresses in and through all creation.

➤ Spirit is all there is, the Creator and Source of an unlimited, abundant and prosperous universe. This abundance flows in, through and as all Life.

➤ There is only one Infinite, unconditionally Loving Intelligence in the universe. This Loving Source is Spirit and It is Cause to all creation.

➤ There is only one Life in the universe, and that Life is Spirit. It eternally lives, moves and has Its Being in, through and as all creation. This Life is ever changing, but never ending. In Spirit, nothing is ever lost, only transformed.

➤ There is only one Creative Power in the universe. This Power is Spirit, and It is unlimited potential, creativity and fulfillment. It fully expresses in, through and as all Life, and It always supports Its expression.

➤ Spirit is the one perfect Creator and Source of Life. It manifests and out-pictures vibrantly in, through and as Its creation, at every level and in every form. In Divine Mind there is a perfect blueprint after which all form is patterned.

❖

STEP 2 - UNIFICATION - "I AM"

➤ I am one with Spirit.

➤ Recognizing this, I therefore realize that I, too, am one with Spirit.

➤ Knowing this, I know that Spirit moves in me, as me and is me. It is my Source, and we are one.

➤ I therefore understand that Spirit is fully and completely present within me, as me now. I am Spirit in perfect expression.

- Spirit's Life is my life now. What is true of It is true of me.

- I therefore recognize that this Intelligence expresses fully through me and as me now. Spirit's Mind is my mind.

- This Life is my life now. Spirit moves in me, as me and is me. There is no separation. It is my source, and we are one.

- And so I recognize that I am perfect Spirit in perfect mind, perfect expression and perfect body.

- As a part of Spirit's creation, I experience my loving oneness with this Infinite Loving Source now.

- I resonate fully with this loving Presence and Power, and feel it manifesting in, through and as me now.

- And so knowing that all that Spirit is, I am, I understand that what is true of It is therefore true of me. I recognize Its attributes and qualities as mine now.

- As a part of creation, I recognize my oneness with *all* creation, and therefore with Spirit. It is my one and only source.

- This Mind/Consciousness/Intelligence/Life is my mind/consciousness/intelligence/life now. It moves, lives and has Its being in me, through me and as me in all ways and in all areas of my life. What is true of Spirit is true of me.

- And as a perfect manifestation of this unlimited Source, I recognize that I am also unconditional love, eternal life, perfect health, unlimited prosperity and supply, and joyous expression.

➤ Knowing that Spirit is all there is, I therefore understand that I am a perfect expression, out-picturing, manifestation and individualization of Spirit. What is true of It is true of me, especially the power of my beliefs, thoughts and words to create my experience and manifest my reality.

❖

TRANSITION STATEMENTS
BETWEEN STEPS 2 & 3

The following are statements that help transition smoothly from Step 2 to Step 3.

➤ And so I speak my word now.

➤ And so from this place of oneness I speak my word.

➤ And so from this consciousness of oneness, I speak my word now.

➤ So as Spirit in perfect expression, I declare my intention now.

➤ And so I speak my word, which, like Spirit's, is Law in the universe.

➤ Recognizing this truth, I speak my word now. I know, declare and affirm that...

➤ From this place of Spirit I recognize the power of my word, and I speak it now.

➢ This perfect Life/Mind/Intelligence is my life/mind/intelligence now. I know, declare and affirm that...

➢ And so from this heightened consciousness/awareness, I speak my word. I know, declare and affirm that...

➢ As part of this Intelligence/Source/Mind/Spirit, I know that my word is Spirit's word, and I declare it now.

➢ And since what is true of Spirit is true of me, I recognize that my word is Law in the universe and I speak it now. I know, declare and affirm that...

➢ And so as Spirit/Infinite Intelligence/Divine Mind/Source in expression right where I am, I know, declare and affirm that...

➢ Knowing that what is true of Spirit is true of me, I recognize that my word, like Spirit's, is powerful. I speak/declare it now.

➢ What is true of Spirit is true of me, especially the power of my word to create my reality. My life is the result of what I believe, think and say. And so I declare and affirm now that...

➢ As a perfect expression of this Higher Power, I *know* that as I firmly speak my intention the Law of Mind has no choice but to manifest my desire now! I make up Spirit's Mind for It where I am concerned. And so I strongly affirm that...

❖

STEP 3 – DECLARATION – "I AFFIRM"

I DECLARE / I AFFIRM
ABUNDANCE / MONEY / PROSPERITY

- The universe is unlimited, endless abundance. I am abundant in all good ways now.

- I am a money magnet. Endless prosperity flows easily to me now and I gratefully accept it.

- Unending prosperity in the form of money easily flows to me, allowing me to more than meet my financial needs, responsibilities and desires.

- As I give, so I receive, and I do both easily, joyfully and freely now.

- I am the perfect flow of giving and receiving. I open to my prosperity and graciously accept it as mine.

- I am prospered in everything I do. All my needs are met now and always.

- I am infinitely and unendingly sustained and supplied in every area of my life.

- And so I recognize that I live in a universe of unlimited abundance, and I gratefully claim my rightful share now.

- Recognizing this truth, I embody the prosperity that is my Divine birthright, and it flows to me freely and effortlessly now.

- Knowing this, I gratefully claim and accept the prosperity that is mine by Divine birthright.

➤ Spirit supports, sustains and supplies me now and at all times.

➤ In this consciousness I allow the unlimited abundance and supply of the universe to flow to me easily and effortlessly now.

➤ I release all old beliefs in lack or limitation and embrace the spiritual truth of unlimited abundance and prosperity that is my Divine birthright.

➤ Knowing that this is so, I accept and embrace the spiritual truth of unlimited abundance and prosperity, and I allow it to manifest fully in my life now.

➤ I recognize that money is a Divine Idea in the Mind of Spirit and I attract all good things, including money, now. I am perfectly sustained and supplied at all times.

➤ Spirit is my only source and supply. I tap into this infinite Source and allow the free, unlimited river of abundance and supply flow to me now.

➤ I release all false thoughts and beliefs that may be keeping me from my rightful abundance/prosperity and allow only a consciousness of infinite, unlimited supply and prosperity to fill my being.

I Declare/I Affirm
Health

➤ I am perfect Spirit, perfect body, perfect health!

➤ Spirit is perfect Life. That Life is my life now. It is a joy to be alive.

➢ I know, declare and affirm that I am perfect Spirit, in perfect form, in perfect health!

➢ In Spirit there is no disharmony or dis-ease. As Higher Power in perfect expression, I deny the power of any condition over me and affirm my perfect wholeness and health now.

➢ Realizing that as a perfect, whole expression of Spirit, in which there is no disharmony or dis-ease, I declare, affirm and express perfect health now.

➢ As perfect Spirit in perfect expression, I affirm that high positive energy, vitality and fitness express in me, through me and as me now.

➢ My body is a Divine Idea patterned after a perfect blueprint in the Mind of Spirit. Any condition unlike this perfection is now lovingly, easily and permanently released. I am perfect health and wholeness now.

➢ Recognizing that Spirit expresses perfectly in and as me, I know and affirm that this perfection also expresses as my perfect health, fitness and vitality.

➢ Knowing that at my core I am Spiritual Perfection and Wholeness, I recognize that this present condition is the result of a false belief and has no power in and of itself. I release this false belief and allow my spiritual perfection to reveal itself in me now, manifesting as perfect health and healing.

➢ I am perfect Spirit in perfect form. Every atom, molecule, tissue, fiber and organ of my being functions at 100% peak performance. All systems work together in perfect harmony. I am whole, healthy and complete.

I DECLARE/I AFFIRM
LOVE/FRIENDSHIP

- Spirit is love. I am loving.

- I live, give and am love in all areas of my life.

- I allow the unconditional, unlimited love and acceptance of Spirit to flow freely through me, as me now, in all my relationships and in all areas of my life.

- Spirit's love is unconditional allowing-to-be. I allow myself to be exactly who I am and am not, and in so doing I allow this for all others.

- The perfect unconditional love of Spirit expresses in me, through me and as me now, returning to me multiplied.

- Expressing the unconditional love of Spirit within me to everyone, I attract that special someone of like mind and spirit now.

- I am perfectly, unconditionally loved because what is true of Spirit is true of me. Knowing that I am accepted as I am, I realize that I can accept others as they are.

- As Spirit individually expressing, I know that I am loved exactly the way I am. I recognize the perfection and divinity of all creation and all people. This love, expressed by means of me, returns to me multiplied a thousand-fold, and I accept it gratefully!

- As a perfect expression of the loving Spirit, I know that love is my true nature. To the degree that I express it, it returns to me multiplied, and I gratefully rejoice in the loving friends and companions who come into my life now.

➤ The unconditional love of Spirit heals all situations or conditions. Allowing this love to flow, I declare this situation healed now.

➤ As an individualization of the Loving Source, I know that the love I seek is already within me. As I accept this, I easily and naturally attract loving, caring people and wonderful friends into my life.

➤ As Spirit Itself in expression, I am unconditionally and completely loved and accepted by the Divine. I allow the experience of it to fill my heart fully.

➤ As a perfect expression of Spirit, I recognize that I am unconditionally loved exactly the way I am. Knowing this for myself, I know and accept it for all people.

I Declare/I Affirm
Work/Self-Expression/Creativity

➤ Spirit is unlimited opportunity, inspiration, creativity and full self-expression. These Divine qualities are mine now, and they flow through me and express as me perfectly.

➤ Knowing this is so, I allow the unlimited creativity and inspiration of Higher Power to flow to me and express as me in all areas and activities of my life.

➤ As Spirit in full expression, I allow myself to do what I love, knowing that the money will follow. My work is appreciated and I am highly compensated.

➤ Aligned with this truth, I attract my perfect new job now and do it with joy, enthusiasm, ease and integrity.

- As a Divine Essence of Spirit, I allow Its Power and Creativity to express fully, effortlessly and joyfully within me and through me in every endeavor and undertaking.

- As perfect Spirit, I recognize that my self-expression is Its expression, and therefore worthy, unique, important and Divine.

- The Universe provides unlimited opportunity. The right and perfect employment exists for me right now, and I attract it easily.

- All channels leading to my perfect work are open and effortlessly revealed to me, and I am guided to it in Divine right timing and order.

- New leads and opportunities for work come to me abundantly. I clearly recognize and act upon them with ease and enthusiasm.

- I welcome and gratefully accept my wonderful new work opportunity, and am highly compensated for satisfying service.

- I allow the Divine Creativity and Self-expression of Spirit to manifest in me as perfect talent and ability in every project I undertake.

- Realizing that I am here to fully and abundantly express Spirit, my life's work is revealed to me clearly and easily now. I recognize and embrace it with joy.

I DECLARE/I AFFIRM
LOSS

➤ Spirit is eternal Life. That Life is my life now.

➤ Spirit is eternal Life. Accepting this, I know that nothing and no one is ever lost, only transformed.

➤ I am an eternal out-picturing and manifestation of Spirit, expressing in an infinite variety of forms, ever evolving and expanding. My Life is never lost.

➤ Since Spirit is Life, It can never be destroyed or lost, only transformed. What we call "death" is only a transition from one form of expression to the next, always upwardly evolving.

➤ Spirit is eternal, and as Spirit in perfect expression, I know that my soul is eternal, for energy can never be destroyed, only transformed. In the infinite scheme of creation, my soul will always live on.

➤ The Life of Spirit, which manifests in, through and as all creation, can never be lost or destroyed, only transformed. Form may change, but Spirit is eternal. I take comfort in knowing that in the infinite scheme of creation, [person's name] will always live on.

➤ Although I grieve the absence of [person's name], I gain comfort knowing that he/she is truly not lost to me. Whether in this present form or not, he/she is an eternal expression of Spirit and continues on in a new and higher form of manifestation.

➤ Knowing that Infinite Intelligence is all there is, I realize that it cannot be destroyed. I take comfort in the realization that the apparent "death" of my mother/father is but a Divine and natural transition to a higher form of expression. She/he will never be lost to me, for her/his essence will remain within and around me always.

➤ Only Spirit can make sense of that which is senseless, as is the death of my child, and I release the "whys" to Spirit. And yet I can take comfort in knowing that Life, as the perfect expression of Spirit, is eternal. I recognize that in the infinite scheme of creation [child's name] lives on in ever higher manifestations of joy and self-expression.

❖

STEP 4 – THANKSGIVING – "I AM GRATEFUL"

➤ Thank you Spirit.

➤ Thank you Divine Loving Source.

➤ I'm so grateful for this truth.

➤ I am filled with thanksgiving for this truth.

➤ And so, knowing that my word is already heard, I give thanks.

➤ Thank you Spirit. I am so grateful, knowing that I am heard now and always.

➤ Knowing that Spirit hears me now and always, I am truly thankful.

➤ Thank you Spirit. I am deeply grateful, knowing that my word is heard now and made manifest even as it is spoken.

> ➤ I am so grateful for this truth, for I know that my word is heard and already in process for immediate manifestation.

> ➤ Recognizing that my word/prayer/affirmation is already a reality in Divine Consciousness, I give thanks.

> ➤ I now give thanks, knowing that my prayer is already made manifest in Divine Mind, where it out-pictures now as my good.

> ➤ Knowing that my word is heard and exists now in Infinite Intelligence, I am grateful. It manifests now as perfect outcome.

> ➤ Thank you Spirit. I am so grateful for this truth. Realizing that my word already exists in Divine Mind, it is now made manifest through the creative process of Infinite Intelligence.

> ➤ How thankful I am for this truth, and I know in faith that my words are now set into motion by the Divine process of Infinite Intelligence.

> ➤ I am filled with thanksgiving for this truth, knowing in faith that my words are already set into motion through the Divine creative process of Infinite Intelligence.

> ➤ Thank you Spirit. I am so grateful for this truth, knowing that my word has already been heard and is even now a perfect idea in Divine Mind. The good I desire is mine now, and I am filled with thanksgiving.

> ➤ I am deeply grateful for this truth, for I know that my prayer is already a perfect idea in the Mind of Spirit.

> ➤ Thank you Spirit. I am deeply grateful for this truth. I know my word is now a perfect blueprint/spiritual prototype in Divine Mind, where it is now in process for immediate manifestation, and for this I give thanks.

❖

STEP 5 ~ RELEASE ~ "I LET GO"

➢ I now let go and let Spirit. And so it is/amen.

➢ I now release my word to Spirit, where it manifests now. And so it is/amen.

➢ I release this word into Divine Mind now where it is immediately manifested for my highest and greatest good. And so it is/amen.

➢ With faith and trust I now release my word into the Law of Mind, knowing that it is already made manifest. And so it is/amen.

➢ I give this word to Spirit now, knowing with faith and trust that my good is already manifesting. And so it is/amen.

➢ I now relax, let go and let Spirit, knowing that my good is already manifesting. And so it is/amen.

➢ And so I release my word into the Law of Mind. I relax, let go and know that it is done. And so it is/amen.

➢ I now release my word into Universal Mind, where through the creative process of Infinite Intelligence it is manifesting now for the highest and greatest good of all concerned. And so it is/amen.

➢ Accepting this truth, I claim it and release it into the Law of Mind, knowing that it is already done. And so it is/amen.

➢ And so with complete faith and trust I release my word into Divine Mind, knowing that it manifests now. And so it is/amen.

➤ With an open, trusting heart I release these words into the Law of Mind, where they are immediately manifested for the highest and greatest good of all concerned. I declare it done. And so it is/amen.

➤ With an open, gracious and trusting heart I release my word into Law, where through Cosmic Consciousness and Infinite Intelligence it is immediately manifested. I let it go and declare it done. And so it is/amen.

➤ And so with the faith and trust *of Spirit* I release my word now into the Law of Mind, where it is immediately manifested for my highest and greatest good, and the highest good of all concerned. I declare it done. And so it is/amen.

CHAPTER TWELVE

AFFIRMATIONS

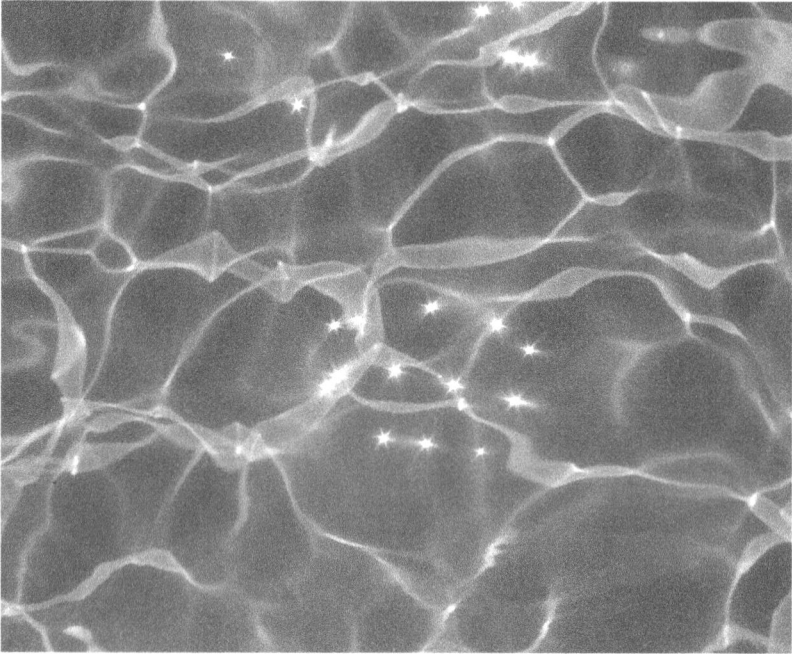

Following are some one and two sentence statements you can say to yourself anytime you need a quick spiritual shot in the arm or pick-me-up. They correspond directly to the five main categories of most concern in people's lives, and can be used as either brief declarations in themselves or incorporated within/added to Step 3. As with the Step Statements discussed in the previous chapter, these affirmations can also be written down on small note or index cards and taken with you for easy reference.

PROSPERITY

➤ Spirit is unlimited prosperity. I am prosperous now.

➤ Spirit within me manifests as my unlimited abundance/prosperity now.

➤ Spirit is infinite supply. I am infinitely supplied in every area and aspect of my life.

➤ Spirit in me manifests and out-pictures as my infinite supply now.

➤ The infinite supply of the Universe flows to me now and always in every good form and in every area of my life.

➤ Wonderful new ways and opportunities for earning, attracting and manifesting income are revealed to me easily and effortlessly now.

➤ Prosperity is my spiritual birthright. I gratefully claim and accept my share now.

➤ Abundance, opulence and prosperity surround me in the form of all creation. I revel, partake and rejoice in the unlimited bounty of the universe.

- ➢ The consciousness of unlimited prosperity within me manifests now as abundant wealth for me. I am a money magnet.

- ➢ The unlimited bounty of the Universe flows to me from all directions and I willingly and effortlessly open myself to receive it now.

HEALTH

- ➢ Spirit within me manifests as perfect health now. I am healthy.

- ➢ My body is patterned after a perfect blueprint in the Mind of Spirit. This perfection reveals and asserts itself now as my perfect physical health.

- ➢ I am patterned after a perfect blueprint in the Mind of Spirit, and anything unlike this perfection is fully, completely and permanently released now. Every particle, atom, molecule, fiber, tissue and organ of my being is saturated in Spirit and functions in perfect harmony and order.

- ➢ As perfect Spirit in perfect expression, I recognize that this present condition has no power in and of itself, does not belong to me, and I willingly, easily and permanently release it now.

- ➢ Spirit is perfect. I am perfect Spirit in perfect mind, perfect form and perfect body.

- ➢ Spirit is well-being. I am perfect well-being. I experience well-being now.

- ➢ Spirit in me manifests as my perfect well-being.

➢ Spirit is wholeness. I am whole and complete now.

➢ The Spirit within me manifests as my perfect wholeness and health now.

➢ Perfect health and wholeness is my spiritual reality, ever present, and any dis-ease or condition is simply obscuring the perfection that is always there. I release this dis-ease/condition now and recognize that my healing is but a revealing.

➢ Healing is a revealing. I clear away and eliminate this false condition and the belief that created it, revealing the perfection, wholeness and health that is there within me now.

LOVE / RELATIONSHIPS

➢ Spirit within me expresses as perfect love now. I am loving and loved.

➢ Spirit is my perfect companion. I am not alone.

➢ As perfect Spirit who sees the Spirit in others, I attract my perfect partner/companion now.

➢ With Spirit everywhere present, I realize that I am not alone. I am surrounded by wonderful friends of like Mind.

➢ Knowing that I am Spirit Itself in perfect expression, I realize that I am my own most perfect companion. I am enough.

➢ Allowing Spirit to express through me, I am the friend I wish to have, the love I wish to attract.

➢ I attract wonderful new people of like Mind to me now.

➢ I allow the love of Spirit to flow and express through me and as me now, and it is reflected back as loving friends and wonderful relationships.

➢ Spirit accepts me unconditionally exactly the way I am and am not. As I recognize this truth, I find that I easily accept others unconditionally too.

➢ Spirit loves and accepts me unconditionally. As I love and accept others unconditionally, I am loved and accepted unconditionally in return.

➢ My relationships are loving, smooth, joyful and harmonious. I attract only those of like Mind, and release those who are not to their highest good.

SELF-EXPRESSION/WORK

➢ Spirit within me expresses as unlimited creativity now.

➢ Spirit in me reveals my perfect purpose now.

➢ Spirit is perfect work. As Higher Power in perfect expression, I attract my perfect work now.

➢ My perfect work/job/income opportunity is revealed to me now in a way that I can clearly see, know, understand and implement.

➢ As a perfect expression of Spirit, I do perfect work. My work is my bliss.

➢ My job/work is easy, effortless and enjoyable, and I do it with love, skill, energy and enthusiasm.

- In this unlimited Universe, employment opportunities abound in all areas, and I attract and create my perfect job now.

- I manifest the perfect job now, in a stimulating, stress-free environment, with like-minded people, perfect benefits and abundant financial compensation.

- I now attract my perfect job, one that is perfectly suited to my talents, temperament and skills, and which I perform with competence, skill and enthusiasm, for which I am highly, abundantly paid.

- I express myself freely with joy, alacrity and enthusiasm, knowing that I am Spirit in perfect expression.

- As Spirit in perfect expression, I am free to be myself with joy, alacrity and wild abandon.

LOSS/GRIEF

- Nothing in Spirit is static, for Life is always in ever-evolving motion. This too shall pass.

- The universe abhors a vacuum, and the loss I am currently experiencing will soon be filled with something greater.

- I allow myself the grief I'm feeling now, knowing that it is a natural expression of Spirit.

- Spirit's nature is joy. I allow it to fill and express in, through and as me now.

- Nothing in Spirit is ever lost, only transformed into its next highest form of expression.

➤ I believe in the infinite soul. Life is eternal, ever manifesting in new and higher forms, always evolving and expanding.

➤ There is no "death", only the eternal transition from one higher form to another.

➤ There is no "death", only eternal Life, evolving, transforming and expanding to ever new and higher forms of expression.

➤ Spirit is Life, and that Life, in all its forms, is eternal. There is no death.

➤ There is no "death", only the endless transformations of eternal Life.

The above affirmations are tailored to be used with the five main human issue categories within Step 3.

❖

The affirmations below address more specific issues. They may also be used within Step 3.

ANXIETY

➤ Spirit is my peace, safety and well-being.

➤ Spirit within me is my peace, confidence, safety and well-being.

➤ Spirit is my peace, safety and well-being, now and in all situations.

➤ I am well-being and peace of mind. All is well. I am safe.

➤ I release all anxiety, worry or concern now, and am filled with the Divine healing peace of Spirit.

➤ I release all anxiety, worry and concern now and replace it with the peace, harmony and serenity of Spirit. I am Divinely guided and protected at all times and in every situation.

BALANCE

➤ I am perfectly balanced now.

➤ Spirit in me manifests as perfect balance and harmony now.

➤ I manifest and experience perfect balance and harmony now in all my thoughts and actions. I am Divinely guided and inspired.

➤ I easily and effortlessly manifest perfect balance and stability in every area of my life and in all my affairs. My life is peaceful, ordered and stress-free.

➤ The universe is a spiritual system of perfect balance and order. As part of it, I allow that balance and order to flow to me and in me now.

➤ The universe is a spiritual system of perfect balance and order. As part of it, I allow that balance and order to flow to me and in me now. My life and all my affairs are stable.

➤ Divine equilibrium and balance flows in me and surrounds me, stabilizing me in all my affairs. My life is ordered and calm.

➤ Spirit is within me. Spirit surrounds me. Spirit is above, below and all around me. My world/life is balanced, calm and stable.

➢ Spirit is within me. Spirit surrounds me. Spirit is above, below and all around me. My affairs are stable and balanced.

CHANGE

➢ I am comfortable with change. I know that I am always Divinely guided and ever expanding my experiences for good.

➢ Change is a universal constant. As one with the universe, I easily and effortlessly ride the wave of change and transformation, knowing that it is a natural universal process and is nothing to fear. Spirit holds me securely in Its grasp, and I am gently guided along my perfect path.

CHOICE

➢ Spirit in me reveals the perfect choice(s) to me now.

➢ Because I am always Divinely guided by Spirit, I know that whatever choice I make is the perfect one, with perfect outcome.

➢ Knowing that I am Divinely guided by Spirit, I am free to choose my experience at any moment.

➢ By means of Infinite Intelligence, the perfect choice is easily and effortlessly revealed to me now.

➢ Knowing that I am Divinely guided and directed by Spirit at all times and in every situation, I confidently make the perfect choice now.

➤ There are no wrong choices. Whatever choice I make, I make it work.

➤ With Spirit to back me, there can be no wrong choices. I make my choice and know it's the right one.

CLARITY

➤ I am perfect clarity!

➤ Spirit in me manifests as perfect clarity now.

➤ As Spirit in perfect expression, I am clear and focused at all times.

➤ Spirit in me manifests as perfect clarity. The solution I seek is revealed now.

➤ I experience perfect clarity now. I know exactly what I need to do and how to do it.

➤ Spirit in me manifests as perfect clarity. All obstacles are eliminated and my way is clear.

➤ As Spirit in perfect expression, the perfect solution to the challenge before me becomes easily and effortlessly clear now.

➤ As Spirit in perfect expression, the perfect solution to the challenge before me becomes easily and effortlessly clear now. I know exactly what to do and how to do it.

➤ I am the clarity and focus of Spirit now. I see and know exactly what I need to do, how to do it, and when.

➤ In Spirit there is no confusion. My vision is clear, my path is free of obstacles and the perfect solution(s) is/are revealed to me now.

➤ The universe is in perfect, Divine clarity and order. It manifests through me, as me, now.

➤ Higher Power now reveals the perfect solution(s) to this/these current challenge(s) in ways that I can clearly see, know, understand and implement.

CONFIDENCE

➤ I am confident!

➤ Spirit is confidence. I am confident.

➤ The unwavering confidence of Spirit fills me now.

➤ Spirit within me manifests as perfect confidence now and in every situation.

➤ The confidence and sureness of Spirit fills and expresses through me, as me and is me now.

➤ I am perfect Spirit in perfect expression. I can do anything I set my mind to.

➤ The absolute confidence of Spirit governs my every action. I have nothing to fear.

➤ Spirit upholds me and enfolds me. It will not let me fall. I face every situation with confidence and certainty.

➤ With Higher Power as my guide, there are no challenges. I move through every situation in my life with faith, confidence and assuredness.

COURAGE

- The courage of Spirit fills me now. I have nothing to fear.

- The Spirit in me manifests and out-pictures as complete courage now and in every situation.

- Through the courage of Spirit within me there is nothing I cannot face or get through. I meet this challenge now with confidence, courage and determination.

- I am filled with the knowing that Spirit directs and protects me. Integrity drives my actions.

- Higher Power is beside me at all times. I feel the fear and do it anyway.

- Spirit supports and guides me at all times. It is within me, around me, above me and below me. I feel the fear and do it anyway, knowing I will emerge triumphantly.

DIVINE RIGHT ACTION

- I claim that Divine Right Action is revealing itself to me now in ways that I can clearly see, know and understand.

- Divine Right Action handles all my affairs and directs every area of my life. I relax, let go, and let Spirit do Its work. There is no need for concern.

- With Divine Right Action to carry and direct me, there is no need for concern. All areas of my life are unfolding perfectly.

➤ Knowing that Divine Right Action pervades every area of my life, I relax with the confidence that I am on my right and perfect path.

➤ Divine Right Action carries me through every area of my life. I relax in the serene knowing that I am on my right and perfect path.

➤ Spirit supports me, sustains me, supplies me and guides me in all situations and circumstances, and in every area and aspect of my life. I am perfectly and Divinely guided every step of the way, at all times.

DOUBT

➤ Spirit is certainty. As Spirit in perfect expression, I am that certainty now.

➤ I release all uncertainty and doubt and allow my Divine inner voice, which is the voice of Spirit, to guide and direct me now.

➤ Spirit knows no doubt. Higher Power shows me what to do, how to do it, and when. I proceed with confidence, clarity and certainty.

➤ I release all feelings of doubt and uncertainty. Knowing that I am Divinely guided by Spirit, I feel sure of myself now!

➤ I release all doubt now! With Spirit to guide me, I am sure of myself and I know what needs to be done. The path I need to take is revealed, and the perfect solution to this situation becomes clear.

➢ In Spirit there is no doubt. Recognizing this truth, I go forth with faith, ease and confidence, knowing that I am Divinely guided and supported in all my endeavors.

➢ Where there is Spirit, doubt has no dominion. I move forward with ease, faith and confidence, knowing that perfect outcomes will result in whatever I undertake.

➢ The mists of doubt within me are cleared away now, revealing the shining light of confidence and peace of mind.

➢ I release all doubt now and allow the certainty, clarity and confidence of Spirit to fill me completely.

➢ With Spirit to back me, I am confident in my thoughts and actions. Whatever choice I make, I know it is the right one.

EASE, SERENITY & PEACE

➢ I am at ease/peace now.

➢ The perfect ease and serenity of Spirit fills me now. All is well.

➢ The perfect peace and serenity of Spirit fills me now. I'm alright.

➢ I release all stress, fear, anxiety and worry now, and allow the serenity and ease of Spirit to fill me completely.

➢ Spirit is within me. Spirit surrounds me. Spirit is above me, below me and all around me. I am at peace.

➢ Everything's alright. With the peace and serenity of Spirit flowing in me, through me and all around me, I know that all is well.

➤ Higher Power protects me. Higher Power sustains me, supports me, supplies me and guides me.

➤ Spirit is within me. It surrounds me and is above, below and all around me. All is well. I am well. I am safe. Spirit protects me. It sustains me, supports me, guides me and supplies me.

FEAR

➤ With Spirit standing for me, who or what can be against me? I have nothing to fear.

➤ Fear is only "false evidence appearing real". What is real is the support, strength and guidance of Spirit manifesting in me, through me and as me now.

➤ In Spirit there is no fear. I move forward knowing that I am Divinely guided, directed and protected, at all times and in all ways.

➤ Spirit protects me. I am safe. Spirit supports me, guides me, sustains me and supplies me, in every area and aspect of my life, in all circumstances and situations, and at all times. I am alright.

PROTECTION

➤ I am Divinely protected at all times.

➤ Spirit shields me. Spirit protects me. I am safe.

➤ The light and love of Spirit shields and protects me always.

- With Higher Power for protection, no harm can come to me.

- I am shielded and protected by Spirit. No harm can come to me.

- Within the protective, enfolding shield of Spirit, I know that no harm can come to me. I am safe.

- The light and love of Spirit shields and protects me now and at all times.

- Spirit enfolds me and upholds me. It shields me and protects me. I am safe.

- The light and love of Spirit shields and protects me now and at all times. I am safe.

- Spirit is within me. Spirit surrounds me. Spirit is above me, below me and all around me. I am safe and protected.

- Spirit is within me. It surrounds me and is above, below and all around me. I am protected. I am safe.

- My Higher Power protects me, sustains me, supports me, guides me and supplies me in every area and aspect of my life, in all circumstances and situations. All is well.

CHAPTER THIRTEEN

STARTING DOWN YOUR
PATH TO PERFECT PRAYING

The following pages are provided so that you can practice writing down your Affirmative Prayers until you familiarize yourself with the five Steps and get the wording just the way you want it. You may wish to use a pencil for easy erasing and modifying. You could just as easily type in a word processor, of course, but writing by hand is a more intuitive, natural way to let the Voice of Spirit flow through you directly onto the paper.

Before beginning, especially if this is your first time, I recommend that you close your eyes, take a few deep breaths and quiet yourself. Get clear in your mind exactly what it is you are praying for. Then begin to write.

The pages after this "practice" section are for you to write down your final Perfect Prayers for whatever issues you like. Refer to and use them as often as necessary, until you manifest the results you desire.

As previously mentioned, once you have composed your Perfect Prayer you can write it on a single sheet of paper, decorative stationery or on note cards. If you feel so inclined, you may wish to copy down all the statements onto individual 3x5 index cards or smaller-sized sheets of loose leaf paper which often come with a binder.

Again, displaying the cards on a small picture-frame easel that you can keep on a desk, dresser or personal altar is also a nice touch. A mini photo album, folding credit card wallet or blank diary are other easy, portable ways you can organize or take your assembled prayer with you to refer to wherever and whenever you wish.

PRACTICE PRAYER

Start with Step 1: God/Spirit/Higher Power, etc. is all there is... He/She/It is... (state some of the qualities or aspects you are praying for)

Step 2: I am one with Him/Her/It... I am (repeat the qualities or aspects of Spirit you listed in Step 1)

Transition Statement: Recognizing this to be true, I declare and affirm that...

Step 3: State whatever it is you are praying for in an affirmative, positive, even assertive manner in the present tense, as if it was already so now and you are simply stating a fact.

Step 4: I am deeply grateful for this truth...

Step 5: And so I release my word now into the Law of Mind... and so it is! (You may add "amen" if you wish.)

Chapter Fourteen

Composing Your Perfect Prayers

MY PERFECT PRAYER FOR:
HEALTH

Step 1:

Step 2:

Transition Statement:

Step 3:

Step 4:

Step 5:

MY PERFECT PRAYER FOR:
ABUNDANCE/PROSPERITY

Step 1:

Step 2:

Transition Statement:

Step 3:

Step 4:

Step 5:

MY PERFECT PRAYER FOR:
LOVE/FRIENDSHIP/RELATIONSHIP

Step 1:

Step 2:

Transition Statement:

Step 3:

Step 4:

Step 5:

MY PERFECT PRAYER FOR:
CREATIVITY/ PERFECT WORK/ JOB

Step 1:

Step 2:

Transition Statement:

Step 3:

Step 4:

Step 5:

MY PERFECT PRAYER FOR:
Loss

Step 1:

Step 2:

Transition Statement:

Step 3:

Step 4:

Step 5:

MY PERFECT PRAYER FOR:

_____

Step 1:

Step 2:

Transition Statement:

Step 3:

Step 4:

Step 5:

AUTHOR'S NOTE

Prayer is an entirely personal and subjective experience. Although the Principles outlined in this book work when properly used, the degree to which they work and the individual results *you* may get will be entirely unique to you. The faith, belief, conviction and *consciousness* with which, and from where, you speak your word will always determine your outcome.

Using the five Steps in this guide may take some practice, especially if you have never used them or prayed affirmatively in this manner before. If at first your results don't seem to be what you'd hoped for, don't give up. *Just keep saying the words.* As you continue doing your spiritual practice you will become more relaxed, more comfortable, more skilled and more confident. Your results will change. As they turn out to look more like what you actually prayed for, your faith in your ability (and, by extension, Spirit's) to manifest through you and for you will grow proportionately. It works if you work it, and what you believe, you can achieve.

It should also be mentioned here that although some outcomes may, *at first*, not look exactly the way you intended, when seen in a larger context, or over a period of time, you may discover that they were, in fact, perfect. For example, praying for income or a new job could manifest as an opportunity to move to another state or country – something you hadn't specifically asked for, or even thought of, but which in the long run, turned out to be exactly what you needed. This happened to me, in fact. Praying for income opportunities brought me to the last place I ever expected to be, South Korea, where I taught English for a year. Where else could someone with *no* teaching experience have found a job that not only paid a decent wage but also provided a rent-free apartment and health benefits? I was even able to *save* money! All that was required of me was that I be a native English speaker and have a B.A. With the skills I already had, the Universe provided me with *exactly* the kind of occupation that most suited my needs at the time. However, it was only over time that I realized this.

Another important point to remember is that Affirmative Prayer is NOT wishful thinking, nor is it passive. Earlier in the discussion of Step 3, a brief mention was made about the appropriateness of being firm when delivering a prayer. Every so often you may find yourself in a situation or circumstance where assertiveness and, yes, even anger is the only way to go. For example, you may have been praying for weeks or months with no satisfying results, and you're at your wits end. You or a loved one might be ill and nothing seems to be working. Or you may find yourself in an extremely stressful or challenging situation and have no clue what to do, feeling helpless. In cases like these, strong emotion can significantly boost the effectiveness of your prayer, so long as it is directed appropriately and does not cause or direct harm to yourself or others. When the occasion warrants it, there is nothing wrong with telling Spirit in no uncertain terms what it is you need, NOW. Instead of saying, "I affirm" or "I declare," shout, "I decree!" or "I demand!" Doing an occasional "goddammit" prayer whenever necessary (aptly named by the aforementioned minister who named Spirit "Big Sweetie") not only kick-starts the Law of Mind into overdrive, it also makes you feel better!

Along with this, the act of *surrendering* can also be very effective, and is in no way an act of weakness or failure. In fact, it is the ultimate act of trust in the Universe. Finding yourself in a situation where you feel helpless, overwhelmed or without any idea what to do, a prayer of surrender, where you release all attempts to try and do it yourself and allow Spirit to take over, can work wonders as far as taking the pressure off yourself and letting (trusting!) the Law of Mind do its work for you. I have had several instances in my life where I've done just that, doing a "goddammit" prayer and then surrendering completely to Spirit, expecting It to show me what to do. It has come through for me every time.

Your word has power, backed by the fuel of your faith, belief and intention. But because Spirit can only work *through* you, once you have stated and released your word, it is then *up to you* to take any necessary and appropriate steps towards fulfilling your goal or desire. Yes, the Universe will certainly create and manifest the perfect opportunities, situations, people or circumstances you need. It will open doorways and clear paths. It will even, if you ask, show you how, when and where. But it is completely up to you to recognize and act upon what is given to you. So if, for example, you are looking for a new job, Spirit can arrange it so that the perfect "help wanted" ad appears in your local newspaper or on a job web site, but it is up to you to do your due diligence. You must buy the paper (or search the web site), look through the Jobs section, find the listing and call the company for an interview.

"Treat and move your feet" is a phrase often used by students of New Thought spiritual science. "Treatment" is another term for Affirmative Prayer. To "move your feet" means to take action and do what you need to do once you've released your prayer. However doing so need not be difficult or effortful. Remember, it isn't necessary for you to move mountains. Once you've released your prayer, Spirit will do that for you. It will show you what you need to do, where you need to go, and what steps you need to take next, one step at a time. It's up to you to take those steps, however. Higher Power will never give you more than you can handle. So, when saying your prayer, particularly during Step 3, also declare that any action you need to take or any process you must go through is smooth, easy and effortless, and that the opportunities or results you are shown are recognizable in ways that you can clearly see, know, understand and implement! You will be amazed at how things seem to fall into place for you, and "moving your feet" will feel more like skating on ice as opposed to slogging through mud!

Spirit is on your side. It always works *for* you, not against you. It lives and expresses in you, through you, as you and *is* you. If what's showing up in your life appears to be negative, then it's only as a result of your consciousness – the Universe simply saying, "Yes" to whatever you're thinking into It. So change your thinking and change your life!

Namaste!

JWL

ABOUT THE AUTHORS

Jon William Lopez, RScP, has been a student of New Thought teachings for over 26 years. He completed his prayer practitioner training in 2006 at the High Desert Center for Spiritual Living in Albuquerque, New Mexico, and received his license in July of 2008. His professional career spans 30 years in the animation industry. He has worked for such studios as Disney Feature Animation, Dreamworks SKG and Film Roman (*The Simpsons*). He recently spent a transformative year in Korea teaching English. His use of Affirmative Prayer has produced miracles in his life, including manifesting his dream jobs, attracting his life partner, and guidance through the care and transitions of his ailing parents.

Jon currently lives in San Antonio, Texas, where he devotes his time to his spiritual growth, photography, writing, digital art, and in service at the San Antonio Center for Spiritual Living.

Jon's work can be viewed at: **www.enlightimages.com** and **www.jonwilliamlopez.com**

❖

Beatrice Elliott, RScP, is a Licensed Prayer Practitioner at the North Hollywood Church of Religious Science in North Hollywood, California. She is also a Speech Pathologist and has her Masters Degree in School Management and Administration. She is the owner and administrator of a private school for Early Education in Agoura Hills, California, the Born Learners School. For more information the school's web site may be viewed at: www.bornlearnersschool.com

In 1995, Ms. Elliott was diagnosed with breast cancer, which marked the beginning of her true spiritual journey. Using the tools of Affirmative Prayer, western medicine, and alternative therapy in her treatment, she is now in perfect health and maintains a consciousness of wellness. As a Licensed Practitioner, Ms. Elliott assists her clients to discover the negative mental causes that may be out-picturing in their life as dis-ease or discord, and to counter and replace negative thoughts with positive affirmations and truthful spiritual statements like the ones found in this book.

Ms. Elliott is currently living in Studio City and is the mother of one son who is in Graduate school at University of California at Santa Cruz.

www.ingramcontent.com/pod-product-compliance
Lightning Source LLC
Chambersburg PA
CBHW031902090426
42741CB00005B/612